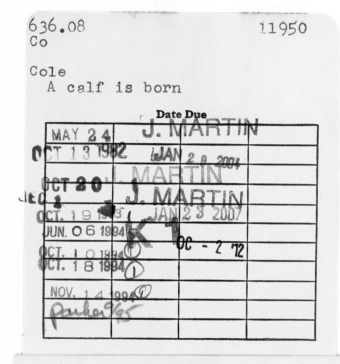

A CALF
IS BORN

by Joanna Cole
with photographs
by Jerome Wexler

William Morrow and Company | New York 1975

Printed in the United States of America.
2   3   4   5   79   78   77   76

Library of Congress Cataloging in Publication Data

Cole, Joanna.
  A calf is born.

  SUMMARY: Describes the habits and characteristics
of a dairy cow and the birth of her calf.
  1. Cows—Juvenile literature.   2. Calves—Juvenile literature.
3. Parturition—Juvenile literature.   [1. Cows.   2. Calves]
I. Wexler, Jerome.   II. Title.
SF208.C64   636.2'1'4   75-12408
ISBN 0-688-22036-3
ISBN 0-688-32036-8 lib. bdg.

The author would like to thank
H. Allen Tucker, Associate Professor,
Department of Dairy Science
at Michigan State University
for his helpful reading of the manuscript.

The photographer wishes to thank
Janet and Bob Self of Field Stone Dairy Farm
of Wallingford, Connecticut,
where this picture series was taken.
He also is grateful for the assistance given him
by Craig Self, Darren Loomis, Sal Greco,
Maria Lagerstorm, and David Findley,
who work on the farm.

Daisy is a milk cow.
She lives on a dairy farm
with 200 other cows.

During the summer,
the cows spend their days
in the pasture.

There is a pond for them
to drink from.
Each cow needs to drink
about twenty-five gallons of water
every day.

There is a salt block
for them to lick.
This salt block has
extra minerals added to it.

And there is plenty of
grass, alfalfa, and clover
for them to eat.

Besides grass, cows like to eat
grains like wheat and corn.
They also eat hay,
which is really grass that has been dried.

Cows have large back teeth for grinding up food.
They have front teeth only on the bottom jaw.
The top jaw has a thick pad instead of teeth.

When a cow eats hay,
she uses her long tongue
to pull it into her mouth.

When she eats grass,
she does not bite it off.
She tears it between her bottom teeth
and the top pad.

Foods like grass and grains are hard to digest.
To help them eat these foods,
cows have a special stomach.

The cow's stomach has four parts.
The first part is called the "rumen."
The rumen is a very large pouch
that can hold fifty gallons of food.
The large rumen makes the cow's sides stick out.

When the cow grazes,
she swallows a great deal of food,
which she hardly chews at all.
This food goes to the rumen,
where special bacteria start to break it down.

When she has eaten and filled the rumen,
the cow lies down to rest.

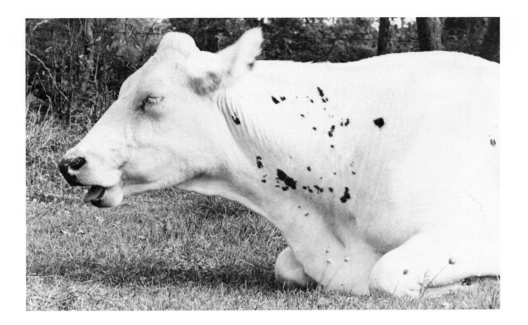

All at once the cow hiccups.
A mouthful of food has come up from the rumen.
The cow chews it very well.
This process is called "ruminating,"
or chewing the cud.

After she has chewed the mouthful,
the cow swallows it again.
This time it does not go to the rumen.
It passes through the second stomach part,
called the "reticulum,"
to the third part, called the "omasum."
In the omasum,
extra water in the food is squeezed out.

Finally the food goes to the fourth part,
called the "abomasum."
This part is the cow's real stomach.
It is like that of animals
with only one stomach.
There the food is further digested
by stomach juices.

Because of her special stomach system,
a cow has to spend a lot of time eating.
Every day she spends about eight hours
just chewing!

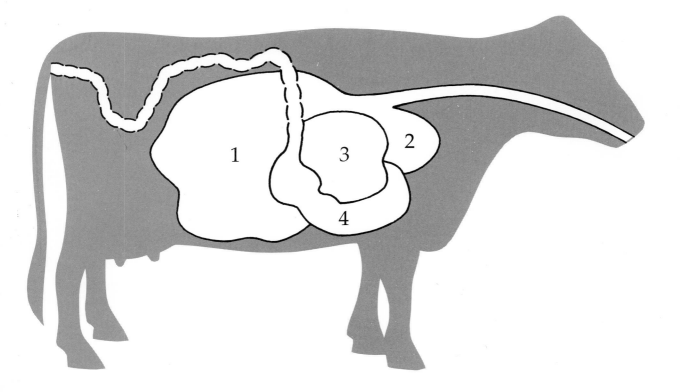

The food that the cow eats
and the water that she drinks
are used to make milk.
The milk is made and stored
in her udder.

A cow is ready to be milked
when her udder is full.

After a day in the pasture,
the cows come home for milking.
They are milked twice a day,
once in the morning
and once in the evening.

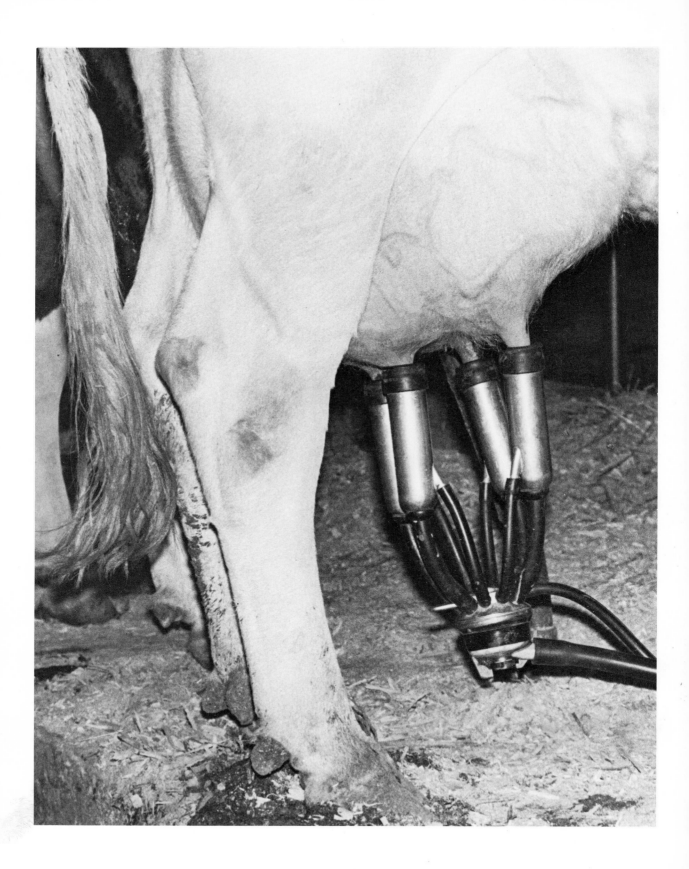

The dairy farmer uses machines
to milk the cows.
Rubber-lined cups fit onto the cows' teats.
A pump pulls the milk from the teats
through hoses into a large tank.
The milking machines do not hurt the cows.
The cows enjoy being milked.

Each cow gives
about five gallons of milk every day.
That amount is enough to fill
sixty-four drinking glasses.

A cow does not produce any milk
until she has had her first calf.
Then she begins to give milk.
In a few months, the farmer has her bred,
and she becomes pregnant again.
The cow will be pregnant for about nine months,
and she keeps on giving milk for most of that time.
Then, shortly before her new calf is to be born,
she has a rest period.

About once a year, Daisy has this rest.
The farmer stops milking her,
and her udder becomes small.

During this time, Daisy is called a "dry" cow,
because she gives no milk at all.
But as soon as her new calf is born,
she will begin giving milk again.

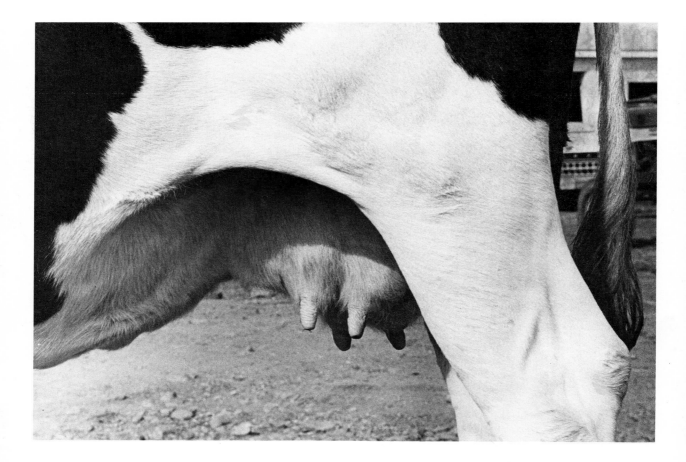

At the end of the pregnancy,
Daisy's calf weighs about 100 pounds
and is ready to be born.

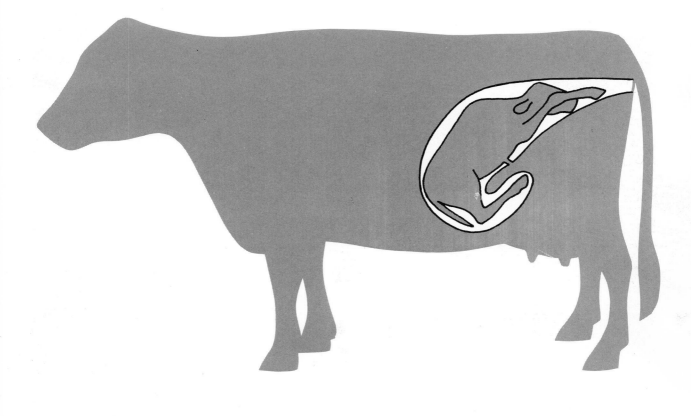

First Daisy goes into labor.
During this stage of the birth,
her muscles push the calf
into the right position to be born.

After a while Daisy lies down.
The unborn calf is inside a transparent pouch
called a "sac."
Now you can see the sac coming out.

The calf's front hooves come out first.
You can see them inside the sac.

Then the head and shoulders follow.
Daisy does not seem to notice what is happening.
Not once has she looked back to see the calf.

As the calf emerges, its front legs move.
They tear open the sac.

Now the calf starts to breathe.

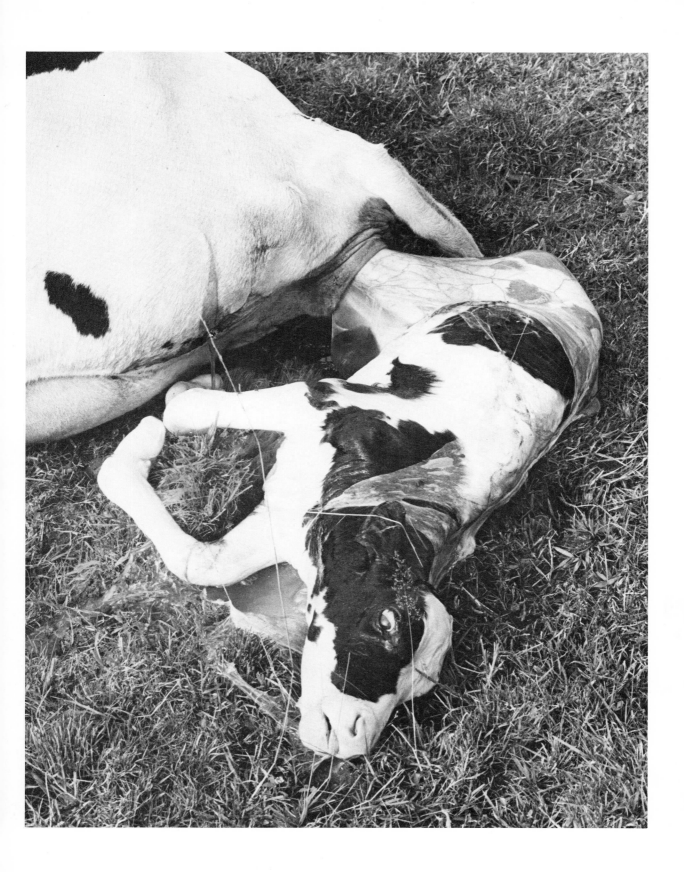

At last Daisy turns to look at her new baby.

The calf moves its head.

Then it raises its head and looks at its mother.
Daisy and her new calf look at each other
for the first time.

The calf is still attached to Daisy
by a tube called the "umbilical cord."
This tube brought food and oxygen to the calf
while it was still in the womb.

When the calf emerges completely,
the cord breaks at a special weak spot.
The place where the umbilical cord was attached
will become the calf's navel.

The cow licks away the sac.
Her tongue cleans and dries the calf.
Her licking helps its blood circulate.

In a few minutes, the calf tries to stand up.

But its legs are still weak,
and it falls on its chin.
It tries again and again,
but it keeps falling down.

Finally it gets to its feet.
It takes a step.

Then it does a little dance.
It seems happy to be up.

The farmer sees Daisy's calf
and names her Speckle.

Speckle is hungry.
She starts looking for her milk.

Is it here? No.

Here? No.

Here? Well, that's close.

At last Speckle finds the teat
and starts to nurse.
Only fifteen minutes have gone by
since she was born!

Daisy's body has made a special yellow milk
for the newborn calf.
This milk is called "colostrum."
It has extra vitamins and protein.
It has antigens to protect the calf from diseases.

Colostrum is not good for people to drink.
It is only good for calves.

After the calf has nursed,
the cow and calf both rest.
In a little while,
the cow's muscles start to push again.
The afterbirth, or "placenta," comes out.
This is the organ that nourished the calf
while it was still in the womb.

Now the placenta is not needed anymore.
Quickly the cow eats it.
Wild cattle do the same thing.
In this way they clean up so that enemies
are not attracted to the new calf by smell.

Speckle stays with her mother for a few days.
Then Daisy's milk changes.
The yellow colostrum is replaced
by ordinary white milk.

Daisy gives much more milk
than Speckle can possibly drink.
She gives enough milk for *six* calves.

Now that she has had her calf
and is giving milk again,
Daisy goes back to be milked
with the other cows.

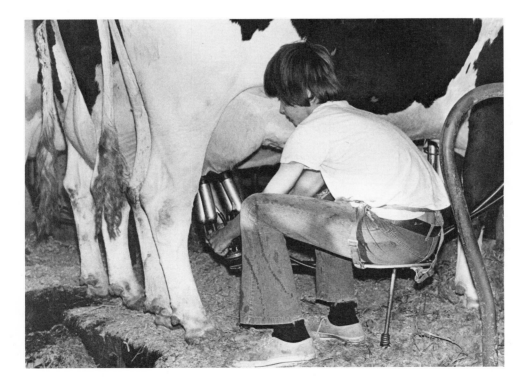

Speckle is put in the calf pen
with other young calves.

At first they are fed a formula
made from skim milk and vitamins.

Then they start eating solid food.

As she grows bigger,
Speckle starts to eat
more and more solid food.
She starts to spend time every day
chewing her cud.

When she is two years old,
Speckle will be old enough
to have a calf of her own.

Then she will be a milk cow,
just like Daisy.